The Clavis or Key: An Exposition of Some Principal Matters and Words in the Writings of Jacob Boehme

Jacob Boehme

Kessinger Publishing's Rare Reprints

Thousands of Scarce and Hard-to-Find Books on These and other Subjects!

- Americana
- Ancient Mysteries
- Animals
- Anthropology
- Architecture
- Arts
- Astrology
- Bibliographies
- Biographies & Memoirs
- Body, Mind & Spirit
- Business & Investing
- Children & Young Adult
- Collectibles
- Comparative Religions
- Crafts & Hobbies
- Earth Sciences
- Education
- Ephemera
- Fiction
- Folklore
- Geography
- Health & Diet
- History
- Hobbies & Leisure
- Humor
- Illustrated Books
- Language & Culture
- Law
- Life Sciences
- Literature
- Medicine & Pharmacy
- Metaphysical
- Music
- Mystery & Crime
- Mythology
- Natural History
- Outdoor & Nature
- Philosophy
- Poetry
- Political Science
- Science
- Psychiatry & Psychology
- Reference
- Religion & Spiritualism
- Rhetoric
- Sacred Books
- Science Fiction
- Science & Technology
- Self-Help
- Social Sciences
- Symbolism
- Theatre & Drama
- Theology
- Travel & Explorations
- War & Military
- Women
- Yoga
- *Plus Much More!*

We kindly invite you to view our catalog list at:
http://www.kessinger.net

THE
CLAVIS,
OR
KEY.

OR,

An Expofition of fome principall Matters, and words in the writings of JACOB BEHMEN.

Very ufefull for the better apprehending, and underftanding of this Booke.

Written in the Germane Language, in March, and Aprill, ANNO. 1624.

BY
JACOB BEHMEN.

Alfo called,
Teutonicus Philofophus.

Printed in the yeare. 1647.

THE PREFACE
TO THE
READER OF THESE WRITINGS

1. IT is written, *The natural man [1]perceiveth not the things of the spirit, nor the Mystery of the kingdom of God, they are foolishness unto him, neither can he know them*: therefore I admonish and exhort the Christian lover of Mysteries, if he will study these high writings, and read, search, and understand them, that he do not read them outwardly only, with sharp speculation and meditation; for in so doing, he shall remain in the outward imaginary ground only, and obtain no more than a [2]counterfeit colour of them.

2. For a man's own reason, without the light of God, cannot come into the ground [of them], it is impossible; let his wit be never so high and subtle, it apprehendeth but as it were the shadow of it in a glass.

3. For Christ saith, *Without me you can do nothing*; and he is the Light of the World, and the Life of men.

[1] understandeth, or receiveth not.

[2] Or feigned shadow of them.

4. Now if any one would search the divine ground, that is, the divine ¹revelation, he must first consider with himself for what end he desireth to know such things; whether he desireth to practise that which he might obtain, and bestow it to the glory of God and the welfare of his neighbour; and whether he desireth to die to earthliness, and to his own will, and to live in that which he seeketh and desireth, and to be one spirit with it.

¹ Or manifestation.

5. If he have not a purpose, that if God should reveal himself and his Mysteries to him, he would be one spirit and have one will with him, and wholly resign and yield himself up to him, that God's spirit might do what he pleaseth with him. and by him, and that God might be his knowledge, will, and ²deed, he is not yet fit for such knowledge and understanding.

² Or working.

6. For there are many that seek Mysteries and hidden knowledge, merely that they might be respected and highly esteemed by the world, and for their own gain and profit; but they attain not this ground, where *the spirit searcheth all things, even the deep things of God*: as it is written.

7. It must be a totally resigned and yielded will, in which God himself searcheth and worketh, and which continually pierceth into God, in yielding and resigned humility, seeking nothing but his eternal native country, and to do his neighbour

service with it; and then it may be attained. And he must begin with effectual repentance and amendment, and with prayer, that his understanding might be opened from within; for then the inward will bring itself into the outward.

8. But when he readeth such writings, and yet cannot understand them, he must not presently throw them away, and think it is impossible to understand them; no, but he must turn his mind to God, beseeching him for grace and understanding, and read again; and then he shall see more and more in them, till at length he be drawn by the power of God into the very depth itself, and so come into the supernatural and supersensual ground, *viz.* into the eternal unity of God; where he shall hear unspeakable but effectual words of God, which shall bring him back and outward again, by the divine effluence, to the very grossest and meanest matter of the earth, and then back and inwards to God again; then the spirit of God searcheth all things with him, and by him; and so he is rightly taught and * driven by God.

9. But since the lovers desire a *Clavis*, or key of my writings, I am ready and willing to pleasure them in it, and will set down a short description of the ground of those strange words; some of which are taken from nature and [1] sense, and [1] *ex sensu*. some are the words of strange [2] masters, which [2] artists, or mystical authors.

* "driven" (*getrieben*), "led, actuated."

I have tried according to sense, and found them good and fit.

10. Reason will stumble, when it seeth heathenish terms and words used in the explanation of natural things, supposing we should use none but Scripture phrase (or words borrowed from the Bible); but such words will not always ply and square themselves to the fundamental exposition of the properties of nature, neither can a man express the ground with them: Also the wise *Heathen* and *Jews* have hidden the deep ground of nature under such words, as having well understood that the knowledge of nature is not for every one, but it belongeth to those only, whom God [1] by nature hath chosen for it.

[1] naturally inclined to it.

11. But none need stumble at it; for when God revealeth his Mysteries to any man, he then also bringeth him into a mind and faculty how to express them, as God knoweth to be most necessary and profitable in every [2] age, for the setting of the confused tongues and opinions upon the true ground again: Men must not think that it cometh by chance, or is done by human reason.

[2] Or *seculum*.

12. The [3] revelations of divine things are opened by the inward ground of the spiritual world, and brought into visible forms, just as the Creator will manifest them.

[3] Or manifestations.

13. I will write but a short description of the divine [4] manifestation, yet as much as I can comprehend in brief; and expound the strange words for

[4] Or revelation.

the better understanding of our books; and set down here the sum of those writings, or a model or epitome of them, for the consideration and help of beginners: The further exposition of [1] it is to be found in the other books.

[1] the divine manifestation, or revelation.

JACOB BEHMEN.

THE CLAVIS OR KEY;

OR,

AN EXPOSITION OF SOME PRINCIPAL WORDS AND MATTERS.

How God is to be considered without Nature and Creature.

14. MOSES saith, The Lord our God is but one only God. In another place it is said, Of him, through him, and in him are all things: in another, Am not I he that filleth all things? And in another, Through his Word are all things made, that are made. Therefore we may say that he is the original of all things: He is the eternal * unmeasurable Unity.

15. For example, when I think what would be in the place of this world, if the four elements and the starry firmament, and also nature itself, should perish and cease to be, so that no nature or creature were to be found any more; I find there would remain this eternal Unity, from which nature and creature have received their original.

* "unmeasurable." In the 1730 edition the word "*unwandlebar,*" "immutable," is added between brackets.

16. So likewise, when I think with myself what is many hundred thousand miles above the starry firmament, or what is in that place where no creature is, I find the eternal unchangeable Unity is there, which is that only Good, which hath nothing either before or after it, that can add anything to it, or take anything away from it, or from which this Unity could have its original: There is neither * ground, time, nor place, but there is the only eternal God, or that only Good, which a man cannot express.

A further Consideration, How this one God is Threefold.

17. The Holy Scripture sheweth us that this only God is [1] threefold, *viz.* one only threefold essence, having three manners of workings, and yet is but one only essence, as may be seen in the outflown power and virtue which is in all things, if any do but observe it: but it is especially represented to us in fire, light, and air; which are three several [2] sorts of workings, and yet but in one only ground and substance.

18. And as we see that fire, light, and air, arise from a candle (though the candle is none of the three, but a cause of them), so likewise the eternal Unity is the cause and ground of the eternal Trinity, which manifesteth itself from the Unity, and bringeth forth itself, *First*, in desire, or will;

[1] Or *triune*.

[2] subsistent forms.

1. Father.
2. Son.
3. Holy Ghost.

* "ground, time nor place," lit., "ground, limit nor place."

Secondly, pleasure, or delight; *Thirdly*, proceeding, or outgoing.

19. The desire, or will is the Father; that is, the stirring or manifestation of the Unity, whereby the Unity willeth or desireth itself.

20. The pleasure, or delight is the Son; and is that which the will willeth and desireth, *viz.* his love and pleasure, as may be seen at the baptism of our Lord Jesus Christ, when the Father witnessed, saying, *This is my [1] beloved Son, in whom I [2] am well pleased; hear ye him.*

[1] Or love.
[2] have pleasure.

21. The delight is the [3] compressure in the will, whereby the will in the Unity bringeth itself into a place and working, wherewith the will willeth and worketh; and it is the [4] feelingness and virtue of the will.

[3] Or impressure of the will.
[4] Or perception.

22. The will is the Father, that is, the stirring desire; and the delight is the Son, that is, the virtue and the working in the will, with which the will worketh; and the Holy Ghost is the proceeding will, through the delight of the virtue, that is, a life of the will and of the virtue and delight.

23. Thus there are three sorts of workings in the eternal Unity, *viz.* the Unity is the will and desire of itself: the delight is the working substance of the will, and an eternal joy of perceptibility in the will; and the Holy Ghost is the proceeding of the power: the similitude of which may be seen in a [5] plant.

[5] Or herb.

24. The [6] *magnet, viz.* the essential desire of

[6] Or loadstone.

nature, that is, the will of the desire of nature, ¹compresseth itself into an *ens* or substance, to become a plant, and in this compression of the desire becometh feeling, that is, working; and in that working the power and virtue ariseth, wherein the magnetical desire of nature, *viz.* the outflown will of God, worketh in a natural way.

[1] Or formeth.

25. In this working perceptibility the magnetical desiring will is elevated and made joyful, and goeth forth from the working power and virtue; and hence cometh the growing and smell of the plant: and thus we see a representation of the Trinity of God in all ²growing and living things.

[2] vegetables, and animate things.

26. If there were not such a desiring perceptibility, and outgoing operation of the Trinity in the eternal Unity, the Unity were but an eternal stillness, a Nothing; and there would be *no nature, nor any colour, shape, or figure; likewise there would be nothing in this world; without this threefold working there could be no world at all.

Of the Eternal Word of God.

27. The Holy Scripture saith, God hath made all things by his eternal Word; also it saith, That Word is God, *John* 1, which we understand thus:

28. The Word is nothing else but the ³outbreathing will, from the power and virtue; a various dividing of the power into a multitude

[3] Or outspeaking.

* "no nature," lit., "no nature nor creature."

of powers; a distributing and outflowing of the Unity, whence knowledge ariseth.

29. For in one only substance, wherein there is no variation or division, but is only one, there can be no knowledge; and if there were knowledge, it could know but one thing, *viz.* itself: but if it parteth itself, then the dividing will goeth into multiplicity and variety; and each parting worketh in itself.

30. Yet because Unity cannot be divided and parted asunder, therefore the separating consisteth and remaineth in the outbreathing will in the Unity; and the separation of the breathing giveth the different variety, whereby the eternal ¹Will, together with the ²Delight and ³Proceeding, entereth into the ⁴knowledge or understanding of infinite forms, *viz.* into an eternal, perceptible, working, sensual ⁴knowledge of the powers; where always in the division of the will, in the separation, one sense or form of the will seeth, feeleth, tasteth, smelleth, and heareth the other; and yet it is but one sensual working, *viz.* the great joyous band of love, and the most pleasant only eternal ⁵Being.

¹ Father.
² Son.
³ Holy Ghost.
⁴ Or science.

⁵ Essence, or substance.

Of the Holy Name JEHOVA.

31. The ancient Rabbins among the *Jews* have partly understood it; for they have said that this name is the highest, and most holy name of God; ⁶by which they understand the working Deity in sense: and it is true, for in this working sense

⁶ Or Jehova is the sensual name of the working Deity.

lieth the true life of all things in time and eternity, in the ground and abyss; and it is God himself, *viz.* the divine working perceptibility, sensation, *[1] invention, science, and love; that is, the true understanding in the working Unity, from which spring the five senses of the true life.

[1] finding knowledge.

32. Each letter in this name intimateth to us a peculiar virtue and working, that is, a form in the working power.

[2] difference, or distinction.
[3] form.

J

33. For I is the effluence of the eternal indivisible Unity, or the †sweet gracefulness of the ground of the divine power of becoming ‡[3] somethingness.

[3] I, I-hood, self, or selfness.

E

34. E is a threefold I, where the Trinity shutteth itself up in the Unity; for the I goeth into E, and joineth I E, which is an outbreathing of the Unity in itself.

H

35. H is the Word, or [4] breathing of the Trinity of God.

[4] Or speaking.

* "invention, science" (*Wissenschaft*), "knowledge."

† "sweet gracefulness" (*Heiligkeit*), "holiness." Both 1682 and 1730 editions have the latter word, but the 1730 has also, in brackets, "*Huldigkeit*," "grace," or "graciousness."

‡ "somethingness" (*Ichheit*), "I-ness," or own-ness; the same applies to the following pars. where the word "somethingness" is used.

O

36. O is the circumference, or the Son of God, through which the I E and the H, or breathing, out-speaketh; from the compressed delight of the power and virtue.

V

37. V is the joyful effluence from the ¹breath-ing, that is, the proceeding spirit of God. [1: Or speaking.]

A.

38. A is that which is proceeded from the power and virtue, *viz.* the wisdom; a subject of the Trinity; wherein the Trinity worketh, and wherein the Trinity is also manifest.

39. This name is nothing else but an out-speaking, or expression of the threefold working of the holy Trinity in the Unity of God. Read further of this in the Exposition of the *Table of the three Principles of the Divine Manifestation.*

Of the Divine Wisdom.

40. The Holy Scripture saith, The wisdom is the breathing of the divine power, a ray and breath of the Almighty; also it saith, God hath made all things by his wisdom; which we understand as followeth.

41. The wisdom is the outflown Word of the

divine power, virtue, knowledge, and holiness; * a subject and resemblance of the infinite and unsearchable Unity; a substance wherein the Holy Ghost worketh, formeth, and modelleth; I mean, he formeth and modelleth the divine understanding in the wisdom; for the wisdom is the passive, and the spirit of God is the active, or life in her, as the soul in the body.

42. The wisdom is the great Mystery of the divine nature; for in her the powers, colours, and virtues are made manifest; in her is the variation of the power and virtue, *viz.* the understanding: she is the divine understanding, that is, the divine [1]vision, wherein the Unity is manifest.

[1] Or contemplation.

43. She is the true divine chaos, wherein all things lie, *viz.* a divine imagination, in which the [2]*ideas* of angels and souls have been seen from eternity, in a divine type and resemblance; yet not then as creatures, but in resemblance, as when a man beholdeth his face in a glass: therefore the angelical and human *idea* did flow forth from the wisdom, and was formed into an image, as *Moses* saith, God created man in his image; that is, he created the body, and breathed into it the breath of the divine effluence, of divine knowledge, from all the three Principles of the divine manifestation.

[2] forms, or images.

* "a subject and resemblance" (*Gegenwurf*), lit., "a counter-throw." Reflection or reproduction, counter-effluence.

Of the ¹Mysterium Magnum.

[1] Or Great Mystery.

44. The *Mysterium magnum* is a subject of the wisdom, where the breathing word, or the working willing power of the divine understanding, floweth forth through the wisdom, wherein also the Unity of God together floweth out, to its manifestation.

45. For in the *Mysterium magnum* the eternal nature ariseth; and two ²substances and wills are always understood to be in the *Mysterium magnum*: the first substance is the Unity of God, that is, the divine power and virtue, the outflowing wisdom.

[2] essences, or beings.

46. The second substance is the separable will, which ariseth through the breathing and out-speaking word; which will hath not its ground in the Unity, but in the mobility of the effluence and out-breathing, which bringeth itself into one will, and into a desire to nature, *viz.* into the properties as far as fire and light: in the fire the natural life is understood; and in the light the holy life, that is, a manifestation of the Unity, whereby the Unity becometh a love-fire, or light.

47. And in this place or working God calleth himself a loving, merciful God, according to the sharpened fiery burning love of the Unity; and an angry ³jealous God, according to the fiery ground, according to the eternal nature.

[3] Or zealous.

48. The *Mysterium magnum* is that *chaos*, out of which light and darkness, that is, the foundation

of heaven and hell is flown, from eternity, and made manifest; for that foundation which we now call hell (being a Principle of itself), is the ground and cause of the fire in the eternal nature; which fire, in God, is only a burning love; and where God is not manifested in a thing, according to the Unity, there is an anguishing, painful, burning fire.

49. This burning fire is but a manifestation of the life, and of the divine love; by which the divine love, *viz.* the Unity, [1] kindleth up, and sharpeneth itself for the fiery working of the power of God.

[1] Or over-inflameth.

50. This ground is called *Mysterium magnum*, or a *chaos*, because good and evil arise out of it, *viz.* light and darkness, life and death, joy and grief, salvation and damnation.

51. For it is the ground of souls and angels, and of all eternal creatures, evil as well as good; it is a ground of heaven and hell, also of the visible world, and all that is therein: therein have lain all things in one only ground, as an image lieth hid in a piece of wood before the artificer doth carve it out and fashion it.

52. Yet we cannot say that the spiritual world hath had any beginning, but hath been manifested from eternity out of that *chaos*; for the light hath shone from eternity in the darkness, and the darkness hath not comprehended it; as day and night are in one another, and are two, though in one.

53. I must write distinctly as if it had a beginning, for the better consideration and apprehension

of the divine ground of the divine manifestation; and the better to distinguish nature from the Deity; also for the better understanding, from whence evil and good are come, and what the [1] Being of all beings is.

[1] Essence of all essences.

Of the [2] Centre of the Eternal Nature.

[2] *Centrum.*

54. By the word [2] centre, we understand the first beginning to nature, *viz.* the most inward ground, wherein the [3] self-raised will bringeth itself, by a reception, into [4] somethingness, *viz.* into a natural working; for nature is but a tool and instrument of God, which God's power and virtue worketh with, and yet it hath its own [5] motion from the outflown will of God: thus the centre is the point or ground of the own receivingness to somethingness; from whence something cometh to be, and from thence the seven properties proceed.

[3] Or own arisen.
[4] I-hood, or I-ness, or own-ness.
[5] Or mobility

Of the Eternal Nature, and its Seven Properties.

55. Nature is nothing but the properties of the receivingness of the own arisen desire; which desire ariseth in the [6] variation of the breathing word (that is, of the breathing power and virtue), wherein the properties bring themselves into substance; and this substance is called a natural substance, and is not God himself.

[6] Or separation.

56. For though God dwelleth [7] through and through nature, yet nature comprehendeth him but so far as the Unity of God yieldeth itself into,

[7] Or throughly inhabiteth, *totaliter.*

and communicateth itself with, a natural substance, and maketh itself substantial, *viz.* a substance of light, which worketh by itself in nature, and pierceth and penetrateth nature; or else the Unity of God is incomprehensible to nature, that is, to the desirous receivingness.

[1] Or consisteth.

57. Nature [1] ariseth in the outflown word of the divine perception and knowledge; and it is a continual framing and forming of sciences and perception: whatsoever the word worketh by the wisdom, that nature frameth and formeth into properties: Nature is like a carpenter, who buildeth a house, which the mind figured and contrived before in itself; so it is here also to be understood.

[2] Or modelleth.

58. Whatsoever the eternal mind [2] figureth in the eternal wisdom of God in the divine power, and bringeth into an *idea*, that, nature frameth into a property.

59. Nature, in its first ground, consisteth in seven properties; and these seven divide themselves into infinite.

The First Property.

[3] Or astringency.

60. The First property is the desire which causeth and maketh [3] harshness, sharpness, hardness, cold, and substance.

The Second Property.

[4] Or pricking.

61. The Second property is the stirring or attraction of the desire; it maketh [4] stinging, breaking, and dividing of the hardness; it cutteth asunder

the attracted desire, and bringeth it into multiplicity and variety; it is a ground of the bitter pain, and also the true root of life; it is the ¹*Vulcan* that striketh fire.

[1 faber, or smith.]

The Third Property.

62. The Third property is the perceptibility and feelingness in the breaking of the harsh hardness; and it is the ground of anguish, and of the natural will, wherein the eternal will desireth to be manifested; that is, it will be a fire or light, *viz.* a flash or shining, wherein the powers, colours, and virtues of the wisdom may appear: in these three first properties consisteth the foundation of anger, and of hell, and of all that is ²wrathful.

[2 grim, fierce, cruel, odious, or evil.]

The Fourth Property.

63. The Fourth property is the fire, in which the Unity appeareth, and is seen in the light, that is, in a burning love; and the wrath in the ³essence of fire.

[3 operation, or property.]

The Fifth Property.

64. The Fifth property is the light, with its virtue of love, in and with which the Unity worketh in a natural substance.

The Sixth Property.

65. The Sixth property is the sound, voice, or natural understanding, wherein the five senses work spiritually, that is, in an understanding natural life.

The Seventh Property.

66. The Seventh property is the subject, or the ¹contence of the other six properties, in which they work, as the life doth in the flesh; and this seventh property is rightly and truly called the ground or place of nature, wherein the properties stand in one only ground.

[¹ compass, conclusion, comprising, or continent.]

The First SUBSTANCE in the Seven Properties.

67. We must always understand two substances in the seven properties: we understand the first, according to the abyss of these properties, to be the divine ²Being; that is, the divine will with the outflowing Unity of God, which together floweth forth through nature, and bringeth itself into the receivingness to sharpness, that the eternal love may become working and sensible thereby, and that it may have something which is passive, wherein it may manifest itself, and be known; and of which also it might be desired and beloved again, *viz.* the ³aching passive nature, which in the love is changed into an eternal joyfulness: and when the love in the fire manifesteth itself in the light, then it *inflameth nature, as the sun a plant, and the fire ⁴iron.

[² Essence, or substance.]

[³ Or painful.]

[⁴ a red-hot iron.]

* "inflameth nature," lit., "inflameth nature and penetrateth it."

The Second SUBSTANCE.

68. The Second substance is nature's own substance, which is [1]aching and passive, and is the tool and instrument of the agent; for where no passiveness is, there is also no desire of deliverance, or of something better; and where there is no desire of something better, there a thing resteth within itself.

[1] painful.

69. And therefore the eternal Unity bringeth itself by its effluence and separation into nature, that it may have an object, in which it may manifest itself, and that it may love something, and be again beloved by something, that so there may be a perceiving, or sensible working and will.

An Explanation of the Seven Properties of Nature.

The First Property.

70. THE First property is a desirousness, like that of a [2]magnet, *viz.* the compression of the will; the will desireth to be something, and yet it hath nothing of which it may make something to itself; and therefore it bringeth itself into a receivingness of itself, and compresseth itself to something; and that something is nothing but a

[2] Or loadstone.

magnetical hunger, a harshness, like a hardness, whence even hardness, cold, and substance arise.

71. This compression or attraction overshadoweth itself, and maketh itself a darkness, which is indeed the ground of the eternal and temporary darkness: At the beginning of the world, salt, stones, and bones, and all such things were produced by this sharpness.

☿ *The Second Property.*

72. The Second property of the eternal nature ariseth from the first, and it is the drawing or motion in the sharpness; for the magnet maketh hardness, but the motion breaketh the hardness again, and is a continual strife in itself.

73. For that which the desire compresseth and maketh to be something, the motion cutteth asunder and divideth, so that it cometh into forms and images; between these two properties ariseth the bitter [1] woe, that is, the sting of perception and feeling.

[1] Or pain.

74. For when there is a motion in the sharpness, then the property is the [2] aching, and this is also the cause of sensibility and pain; for if there were no sharpness and motion, there would be no sensibility: this motion is also a ground of the air in the visible world, which is manifested by the fire, as shall be mentioned hereafter.

[2] Or painful.

75. Thus we understand that the desire is the ground of somethingness, so that something may

come out of nothing; and thus we may also conceive that the desire hath been the beginning of this world, by which God hath brought all things into substance and being; for the desire is that by which God said, ¹*Let there be.* The desire is that *Be it,* which hath made something where nothing was, but only a spirit; it hath made the *Mysterium magnum* (which is spiritual) visible and substantial, as we may see by the elements, stars, and other creatures. [1] Or *Fiat.*

76. The Second property, that is, the ²motion, was in the beginning of this world the separator or divider in the powers and virtues, by which the Creator, *viz.* the will of God, brought all things out of the *Mysterium magnum* into form; for it is the outward movable world, by which the supernatural God made all things, and brought them into form, figure, and ³shape. [2] Or stirring. [3] Or images.

⚥ *The Third Property.*

77. The Third property of the eternal nature is the anguish, *viz.* that ⁴will which hath brought itself into the receivingness to nature and somethingness: when the own will standeth in the sharp motion, then it cometh into anguish, that is, into sensibility; for without nature it is not feelable, but in the movable sharpness it becometh feeling. [4] Or *Velle.*

78. And this feelingness is the cause of the fire, and also of the mind and senses; for the own

natural will is made volatile by it, and seeketh rest; and thus the separation of the will goeth out from itself, and pierceth through the properties, from whence the taste ariseth, so that one property tasteth and feeleth the other.

79. It is also the ground and cause of the senses, in that one property penetrateth into the other, and kindleth the other, so that the will knoweth whence the passiveness cometh; for if feeling were not, the will could know nothing of the properties, for it were alone: and thus the will receiveth nature into it, by feeling the sharp motion in itself.

80. This motion is in itself like a turning wheel; not that there is such a turning and winding, but it is so in the properties; for the desire attracteth into itself, and the motion thrusteth forwards out of itself, and so the will, being in this anguish, can neither get inwards nor outwards, and yet is drawn both out of itself and into itself; and so it remaineth in such a [1] posture, as would go into itself and out of itself, that is, over itself and under itself, and yet can go no whither, but is an anguish, and the true foundation of hell, and of God's anger; for this anguish standeth in the dark sharp motion.

[1] form, manner, or condition.

81. In the creation of the world the sulphur-spirit, with the matter of the sulphureous [2] nature, was produced out of this ground; which sulphur-spirit is the natural life of the earthly and elementary creatures.

[2] Or property.

82. The wise heathen have in some measure understood this ground, for they say, that in ¹*Sulphur*, ²*Mercury*, and ³*Sal*, all things in this world consist; wherein they have not looked upon the matter only, but upon the spirit, from which such matter proceedeth: for the ground of it consisteth not *in salt, quicksilver, and brimstone, they mean not so, but they mean the spirit of such properties; in that, everything indeed consisteth, whatsoever liveth and groweth and hath being in this world, whether it be spiritual or material.

¹ Spiritual corporality.
² The word, or speaking.
³ The gross palpable corporality.

83. For they understand by *Salt*, the sharp magnetical desire of nature; and by *Mercury*, they mean the motion and separation of nature, by which everything is ⁴figured with its own signature; and by *Sulphur*, they mean the perceiving [sensible] ⁵willing and growing life.

⁴ Or marked with its own image, or shape.
⁵ desiring vegetable life.

84. For in the sulphur-spirit, wherein the fiery life burneth, the oil lieth; and the quintessence lieth in the oil, *viz.* the fiery *Mercury*, which is the true life of nature, and which is an effluence from the word of the divine power and motion, wherein the ground of heaven is understood; and in the quintessence there lieth the tincture, *viz.* the paradisical ground, the outflown word of the divine power and virtue, wherein the properties lie in ⁶equality.

⁶ temperature or harmony.

85. Thus, by the Third property of nature, which is the anguish, we mean the sharpness and

* "in salt" (*im groben sale*), "in gross salt."

painfulness of the fire, *viz.* the burning and consuming; for when the will is put into such a sharpness it will always consume the cause of that sharpness; for it always **¹striveth to get to the Unity of God again, which is the rest; and the Unity thrusteth itself with its effluence to this motion and sharpness; and so there is a continual conjoining for the manifestation of the divine will, as we always find in these three, *viz.* in salt, brimstone, and oil, a heavenly in the earthly; and whosoever doth but truly understand it, and considereth the spirit, shall find it so.

[1] Or throngeth after.

86. For the soul of a thing lieth in the sharpness, and the true life of the sensual nature and property lieth in the motion, and the powerful spirit which ariseth from the tincture lieth in the oil of the *Sulphur*: Thus a heavenly always lieth hidden in the earthly, for the invisible ²spiritual world came forth with and in the creation.

[2] *Viz.*, the light and dark world; God's love and wrath.

☉ *The Fourth Property.*

87. The Fourth property of the eternal nature is the spiritual fire, wherein the light, that is, the Unity, is made manifest; for the ³glance of the fire ariseth and proceedeth from the outflown Unity, which hath incorporated and united itself with the natural desire; and the burning property

[3] shining lustre or brightness.

---

* "striveth," "throngeth after," "thrusteth itself"; these are renderings of the one word "*dringen*," which implies an urge, a forceful penetration.

of fire, *viz.* the heat proceedeth from the sharp devouringness of the first three properties; which cometh to be so as followeth.

88. The eternal Unity (which I also in some of my writings call the liberty) is the soft and still tranquillity, being amiable, and as a soft comfortable ease, and it cannot be expressed how soft a tranquillity there is without nature in the Unity of God; but the three properties (in order) to nature are sharp, painful, and horrible.

89. In these three painful properties the outflown will *consisteth, and is produced by the Word or divine breathing, and the Unity also is therein; therefore the will longeth earnestly for the Unity, and the Unity longeth for the sensibility, *viz.* for the fiery ground: thus the one longeth to get into the other; and when this longing is, there is as it were a ¹cracking noise or flash of lightning, as when we strike steel and a stone together, or pour water into fire: this we speak by way of similitude. [¹ crashing.]

90. In that flash the Unity feeleth the sensibility, and the will receiveth the soft tranquil Unity; and so the Unity becomes a shining glance of fire, and the fire becometh a burning love, for it receiveth ²the *ens* and power from the soft Unity: in this kindling the darkness of the magnetical compressure is †pierced through with the light, so [² Or entity.]

---

* "consisteth" (*stehet*), "stands," or "is."
† "pierced through" (*durchdrungen*), "penetrated," or "permeated."

that it is no more known or discerned, although it remaineth in itself eternally in the compressure.

91. Now two eternal Principles arise here, *viz.* the darkness, harshness, sharpness, and pain dwelling in itself; and the feeling, power and virtue of the Unity in the light; upon which the scripture saith, that God (that is, the eternal Unity) dwelleth in a light to which none can [1] come.

[1] Or approach.

92. For so the eternal Unity of God manifesteth itself through the spiritual fire, in the light, and this light is called Majesty; and God (that is, the supernatural Unity) is the power and virtue of it.

93. For the spirit of this fire receiveth *ens* [or virtue] to shine, from the Unity, or else this fiery [2] ground would be but a painful, horrible hunger, and pricking desire; and it is so indeed, when the will breaketh itself off from the Unity, and will live after its own desire, as the devils have done, and the false soul still doth.

[2] Or spirit.

94. And thus you may here perceive two Principles: the first is the ground of the burning of the fire, *viz.* the sharp, moving, perceivable, painful darkness in itself; and the second is the light of the fire, wherein the Unity cometh into mobility and joy; for the fire is * an object of the great love of God's Unity.

95. For so the eternal delight becometh perceivable, and this perceiving of the Unity is called

* "an object" (*ein Gegenwurf*); see *, p. 8.

love, and is a burning or life in the Unity of God; and according to this burning of love, God calleth himself a merciful loving God; for the Unity of God loveth and pierceth through the [1] painful will of the fire (which at the beginning arose in the breathing of the word, or outgoing of the divine delight), and changeth it into great joy.

[1] aching.

96. And in this fiery will of the eternal nature standeth the soul of man, and also the angels; this is their ground and centre; therefore, if any soul breaketh itself off from the light and love of God, and entereth into its own natural desire, then the ground of this darkness and painful [2] property will be manifest in it; and this is the hellish fire, and the anger of God, when it is made manifest, as may be seen in *Lucifer*; and whatsoever can be thought to have a being [3] anywhere in the creature, the same is likewise without the creature everywhere; for the creature is nothing else but an image and figure of the separable and various power and virtue of the universal Being.

[2] Or source.

[3] Or everywhere.

97. Now understand aright what the ground of fire is, *viz.* cold from the compressure, and heat from the anguish; and the motion is the [4] *Vulcan*; in these three the fire consisteth, but the shining of the light ariseth and proceedeth from the conjunction of the Unity in the ground of fire, and yet the whole ground is but the outflown will.

[4] Or striker of fire.

98. Therefore in fire and light consisteth the life of all things, *viz.* in the will thereof, let them

be ¹insensible, *vegetable, or rational things; everything, as the fire, hath its ground, either from the eternal, as the soul, or from the temporary, as astral elementary things; for the eternal is one fire, and the temporary is another, as shall be shewn hereafter.

¹ Or inanimate, or dumb.

♀ *The Fifth Property.*

99. Now the Fifth property is the fire of love, or the ²world of power and light; which in the darkness dwelleth in itself, and the darkness comprehendeth it not, as it is written, *John* i. *The light shineth in the darkness, and the darkness comprehendeth it not*: Also, the Word is in the light, and in the Word is the true understanding life of man, *viz.* the true spirit.

² power and light world.

100. But this fire is the true soul of man, *viz.* the true spirit, which God breathed into man for a creaturely life.

101. You must understand, in the spiritual fire of the will, the true desirous soul out of the eternal ground; and in the power and virtue of the light, the true understanding spirit, in which the Unity of God dwelleth and is manifest, as our Lord Christ saith, ³*The kingdom of God is within you*; and *Paul* saith, ⁴*Ye are the temple of the Holy Ghost, who dwelleth in you*; this is the place of the divine inhabiting and revelation.

³ Luke xvii. 21.
⁴ 1 Cor. vi. 19.

102. Also the soul cometh to be damned thus:

* "vegetable" (*wachsenden*), "growing."

when the fiery will breaketh itself off from the love and Unity of God, and entereth into its own natural propriety, that is, into its evil properties. This ought further to be considered.

103. O Zion, observe this ground, and thou art freed from *Babel*!

104. The second Principle (*viz.* the angelical world and the thrones) is meant by the fifth property: for it is the motion of the Unity, wherein all the properties of the fiery nature burn in love.

105. An example or similitude of this ¹ground [1: Or thing.] may be seen in a candle that is lighted. The properties lie in one another in the candle, and none of them is more manifested than another, till the candle be lighted; and then we find fire, oil, light, air, and water from the air: all the four elements become manifest in it, which lay hidden before in one only ground.

106. And so likewise it must be conceived to be in the eternal ground; for the temporary substance is flown forth from the eternal, therefore they are both of the same quality; but with this difference, that one is eternal and the other transitory, one spiritual and the other corporeal.

107. When the spiritual fire and light shall be kindled, which hath indeed burned from eternity [in itself], then shall also the Mystery of the divine power and knowledge be always made manifest therein; for all the properties of the eternal nature

become spiritual in the fire, and yet nature remaineth as it is, inwardly in itself; and the going forth of the will becometh spiritual.

108. For in the [1]crack or flash of the fire the dark receptibility is consumed; and in that consuming, the pure bright fire-spirit, which is pierced through with the glance of the light, goeth forth; in which going forth we find three several properties.

[1] hissing, or noise.

109. The first is the going upwards of the fiery will; the second is the going downwards, or sinking of the watery spirit, viz. the meekness; and the third is the going out forwards of the oily spirit, in the midst, in the centre of the fiery spirit of the will; which oily spirit is the *ens* of the Unity of God, which is become a substance in the desire of nature; yet all is but spirit and power: but so it appears in the figure of the manifestation, not as if there were any severing or division, but it appears so in the manifestation.

110. This threefold manifestation is according to the Trinity; for the centre wherein it is, is the only God according to his manifestation: the fiery flaming spirit of love is that which goeth upwards, and the meekness which proceedeth from the love is that which goeth downwards, and in the midst there is the centre [[2]of] the circumference, which is the Father, or whole God, according to his manifestation.

[2] or.

111. And as this is to be known in the divine manifestation, so it is also in the eternal nature,

according to nature's property; for nature is but a *[1] resemblance of the Deity.

[1] picture, representation, or shadow.

112. Nature may be further considered thus: the flash of the original of fire is a crack, and salnitrous ground, whence nature goeth forth into infinite divisions, that is, into multitudes or varieties of powers and virtues; from which the multitude of angels and spirits, and their colours and operations proceeded, also the four elements in the beginning of time.

113. For the [2] temperature of fire and light is the holy element, *viz.* the motion in the light of the Unity; and from this salnitrous ground (we mean spiritual, not earthly salnitre) the four elements proceed, *viz.* in the [3] compressure of the fiery *Mercury*, earth and stones are produced; and in the quintessence of the fiery *Mercury*, the fire and heaven; and in the motion or going forth, the air; and in the disruption or rending of the desire by the fire, the water is produced.

[2] temperament, or harmony.

[3] Compressure or impressure, in every place where that word is used, following.

114. The fiery *Mercury* is a dry water, that hath brought forth metals and stones; but the broken or divided *Mercury* hath brought forth wet water, by the mortification in the fire; and the compressure hath brought the gross rawness into the earth, which is a gross salnitrous Saturnine *Mercury*.

115. By the word *Mercury*, you must understand

* "resemblance" (*Gegenwurf*); see *, p. 8.

here, in the spirit, always the outflown natural working Word of God, which hath been the separator, divider, and former of every substance; and by the word *Saturn*, we mean the compressure.

116. In the fifth property, that is, in the light, the eternal Unity is substantial; that is, a holy spiritual fire, a holy light, a holy air, which is nothing else but spirit, also a holy water, which is the outflowing love of the Unity of God, and a [1] holy earth, which is all-powerful virtue and working.

[1] *ternarium sanctum.*

117. This fifth property is the true spiritual angelical world of the divine joy, which is hidden in this visible world.

♃ *The Sixth Property.*

118. The Sixth property of the eternal nature is the sound, noise, voice, or understanding; for when the fire flasheth, all the properties together sound: the fire is the mouth of the essence, the light is the spirit, and the sound is the understanding wherein all the properties understand one another.

119. According to the manifestation of the holy Trinity, by the effluence of the Unity, this sound or voice is the divine working word, *viz.* the understanding in the eternal nature, by which the supernatural knowledge manifesteth itself; but according to nature and creature, this sound or voice is the knowledge of God, wherein the natural

understanding knoweth God; for the natural understanding is *a platform, resemblance, and effluence from the divine understanding.

120. The five senses lie in the natural understanding, in a spiritual manner, and in the second property (*viz.* in the motion in the fiery *Mercury*) they lie in a natural manner.

121. The sixth property giveth understanding in the voice or sound, *viz.* in the ¹speaking of the word; and the second property of nature is the producer, and also the house, tool, or instrument of the speech or voice: in the second property the power and virtue is painful; but in the sixth property it is joyful and pleasant; and the difference between the second and sixth property is in light and darkness, which are in one another, as fire and light; there is no other difference between them.

¹ articulation.

☾ *The Seventh Property.*

122. The Seventh property is the substance, that is, the *subjectum* or house of the other six, in which they all are substantially as the soul in the body: by this we understand especially, as to the light-world, the paradise or budding of the working power.

123. For every property maketh unto itself a †subject, or ²object, by its own effluence; and in

² Or resemblance.

---

* "a platform," etc. (*Gegenwurf*); see *, p. 8.

† "subject or object" (*Gegenwurf*); see *, p. 8.

the seventh all the properties are in a temperature, as in one only substance: and as they all did proceed from the Unity, so they all return again into one ground.

124. And though they work in different kinds and manners, yet here there is but one only substance, whose power and virtue is called tincture; that is, a holy penetrating, growing or springing * bud.

125. Not that the seventh property is the tincture, but it is the ¹body of it; the power and virtue of the fire and light is the tincture ²in the substantial body: but the seventh property is the substance which the tincture †penetrateth and sanctifieth; we mean, that it is thus according to the power and virtue of the divine manifestation; ‡but as it is a property of nature, it is the substance of the attracted desire of all properties.

¹ *corpus aut substantia.*
² Or with.

126. It is especially to be ³observed, that always the First and the Seventh property are accounted for one; and the Second and Sixth; also the Third and Fifth; and the Fourth is only the dividing mark or ⁴bound.

³ See the Table following.
⁴ Or limit.

127. For according to the manifestation of the Trinity of God, there are but three properties of

* "bud" (*Wesen*), essence or being.

† "penetrateth and sanctifieth." The original proceeds: "therefore paradise is [consists in] a spiritual budding in the seventh property."

‡ "but as it is," etc., lit., "but, as a property of nature, it is," etc.

nature: the first is the desire which belongeth to God the Father, yet it is only a spirit; but in the seventh property the desire is substantial.

128. The second is the divine power and virtue, and belongeth to God the Son; in the second number it is only a spirit; but in the sixth it is the substantial power and virtue.

129. The third belongeth to the Holy Ghost; and in the beginning of the third property it is only a fiery spirit; but in the fifth property the great love is manifested therein.

130. Thus the effluence of the divine manifestation, as to the three properties in the first Principle before the light,[1] is natural; but in the second Principle in the light it is spiritual.

[1] appeareth.

131. Now these are the seven properties in one only ground; and all seven are equally eternal without beginning; none of them can be accounted the first, second, third, fourth, fifth, sixth, or last; for they are equally eternal without beginning, and have also one eternal beginning from the Unity of God.

132. We must represent this in a typical way, that it may be understood how the one is born out of the other, the better to conceive what the Creator is, and what the life and substance of this world is.

The Seven Forms of Spirits, mentioned Revel. Chap. 1.

♄	The First	Harsh Desiring Will
☽	Second	Bitter or Stinging
♃	Third	Anguish, till the Flash of Fire
☿	Fourth	Fire { Dark-Fire / Light-Fire } Form
☉		
♂	Fifth	Light or Love, whence the water of Eternal Life floweth
♀	Sixth	Noise, Sound, or Mercury
♄	Seventh	Substance or Nature

The First Principle.

⎰ 1. **Dark-World**; a similitude of it is a candle.

The Dark-World; hence God the Father is called an Angry, Zealous, Jealous God, and a Consuming Fire. } **Dark or Fire of Wrath**

⎱ 2. **Fire-World**; a similitude of it is the fire of a candle.

The Second Principle.

⎰ 3. **Light-World**; a similitude of it is the light of a candle.

The Light-World; hence God the Son, the Word, the Heart of God, is called a Loving and Merciful God. } **Light or Fire of Love**

The Third Principle.

This World of four Elements, which is produced out of the two Inward Worlds, and is a Glass of them; wherein Light and Darkness, Good and Evil are mixed, it is not Eternal, but hath a Beginning and an End.

Of the Third Principle, viz. The Visible World; whence that proceeded; and what the Creator is.

133. THIS visible world is sprung from the spiritual world before mentioned, *viz.* from the outflown divine power and virtue; and it is a * subject or object resembling the spiritual world: the spiritual world is the inward ground of the visible world; the visible subsisteth in the spiritual.

134. The visible world is only an effluence of the seven properties, for it proceeded out of the six working properties; but in the seventh (that is, in paradise) it is in rest: and that is the eternal Sabbath of rest, wherein the divine power and virtue resteth.

135. *Moses* saith, God created heaven and earth, and all creatures, in six days, and rested on the seventh day, and also commanded [1] it to be kept for a rest.

[1] Or to rest on it.

136. The understanding lieth hidden and secret in those words. Could not he have made all his works in one day? Neither can we properly say there was any day before the sun was; for in the deep there is but one day [in all].

137. But the understanding lieth hidden in those words. He understandeth by each day's working, the creation or manifestation of the seven properties; for he saith, In the beginning God created heaven and earth.

* "subject or object" (*Gegenwurf*); see *, p. 8.

138. In the FIRST ¹motion, the magnetical desire compressed and compacted the fiery and watery *Mercury* with the other properties; and then the grossness separated itself from the spiritual nature: and the fiery became metals and stones, and partly salnitre, that is, earth: and the watery became water. Then the fiery *Mercury* of the working became clean, and *Moses* calleth it heaven; and the Scripture saith, God dwelleth in heaven: for this fiery *Mercury* is the power and virtue of the firmament, *viz.* an image and resemblance of the spiritual world, in which God is manifested.

139. When this was done, God said, Let there be light; then the inward thrust itself forth through the fiery heaven, from which a shining power and virtue arose in the fiery *Mercury*, and that was the light of the outward nature in the properties, wherein the ²vegetable life consisteth.

¹ The first day.
² Or growing.

The Second Day.

140. In the SECOND day's work, God separated the watery and fiery *Mercury* from one another, and called the fiery the firmament of Heaven, which came out of the midst of the waters, *viz.* of *Mercury*, whence arose the male and female ³kind, in the spirit of the outward world; that is, the male in the fiery *Mercury*, and the female in the watery.

141. This separation was made all over in everything, to the end that the fiery *Mercury* should desire and long for the watery, and the watery

³ sex.

for the fiery; that so there might be a desire of love betwixt them in the light of nature, from which the conjunction ariseth: therefore the fiery *Mercury*, viz. the outflown word, separated itself according both to the fiery and to the watery nature of the light, and thence comes both the male and female kind in all things, both animals and vegetables.

The Third Day.

142. In the THIRD day's work, the fiery and watery *Mercury* entered again into conjunction or mixture, and embraced one another, wherein the salnitre, *viz.* the separator in the earth, brought forth grass, plants, and trees; and that was the first generation or production between male and female.

The Fourth Day.

143. In the FOURTH day's work the fiery *Mercury* brought forth its fruit, *viz.* the fifth essence, a higher power or virtue of life than the four elements, and yet it is in the elements: of it the stars are made.

144. For as the compression of the desire brought the earth into a [1] mass, the compressure entering into itself, so the fiery *Mercury* thrust itself outwards by the compressure, and hath enclosed the place of this world with the [2] stars and starry heaven.

[1] Or lump.

[2] Or constellations.

The Fifth Day.

145. In the FIFTH day's work the [1]*spiritus mundi*, that is, the [2]soul of the great world, opened itself in the fifth essence (we mean the life of the fiery and watery *Mercury*); therein God created all beasts, fishes, fowls, and worms; every one from its peculiar property of the divided *Mercury*.

146. Here we see how the eternal Principles have moved themselves according to evil and good, as to all the seven properties, and their effluence and mixture; for there are evil and good creatures created, everything as the *Mercury* (that is, the separator) hath figured and [3]framed himself into an *ens*, as may be seen in the evil and good creatures: And yet every kind of life hath its original in the light of nature, that is, in the love of nature; from which it is that all creatures, in their kind or property, love one another according to this outflown love.

[1] spirit of the world.
[2] *anima macrocosmi.*
[3] Or imaged.

The Sixth Day.

147. In the SIXTH day's work, God created man; for in the sixth day the understanding of life opened itself out of the fiery *Mercury*, that is, out of the inward ground.

148. God created him in his likeness, out of all the three Principles, and made him an image, and breathed into him the understanding fiery *Mercury*, according to both the inward and outward ground,

that is, according to time and eternity, and so he became a living understanding soul: and in this ground of the soul, the manifestation of the divine holiness did move, *viz.* the living outflowing Word of God, together with *the eternal knowing *idea*, which was known from eternity in the divine wisdom, as a subject or form of the divine imagination.

149. This [1]*idea* becomes [2]clothed with the substance of the heavenly world, and so it becometh an understanding spirit and temple of God; an image of the divine [3]vision, which spirit is given to the soul for a spouse: as fire and light are espoused together, so it is here also to be understood.

[1] Or image.
[2] endued, or invested.
[3] Or contemplation.

150. This divine ground budded and pierced through soul and body; and this was the true paradise in man, which he lost by sin, when the ground of the dark world, with the false desire, gat the upper hand and dominion in him.

The Seventh Day.

151. In the SEVENTH day God rested from all his works which he had made, saith *Moses*; yet God needeth no rest, for he hath wrought from eternity, and he is a mere working power and virtue; therefore the meaning and understanding here lieth hidden in the word, for *Moses* saith

* "the eternal knowing idea," lit., "the eternally known idea."

he hath commanded [us] to rest on the seventh day.

152. The seventh day was the true paradise (understand it spiritually), that is, the tincture of the divine power and virtue, which is a temperament; this pierced through all the properties, and wrought in the seventh, that is, in the substance of all the other.

153. The tincture pierced through the earth, and through all elements, and tinctured all; and then paradise was on earth, and in man; for evil was hidden: as the night is hidden in the day, so the [1] wrath of nature was also hidden in the first Principle, till the fall of man; and then the divine working, with the tincture, [2] fled into their own Principle, *viz.* into the inward ground of the light-world.

[1] Or grim fierceness.

[2] Or retired.

154. For the [1] wrath arose aloft, and got the predominancy, and that is the curse, where it is said, God cursed the earth; for his cursing is to leave off and fly from his working: as when God's power and virtue in a thing worketh with the life and spirit of the thing, and afterwards withdraweth itself with its working; then the thing is cursed, for it worketh in its own will, and not in God's will.

Of the Spiritus Mundi, *and of the Four Elements.*

155. We may very well observe and consider the hidden spiritual world by the visible world:

for we see that fire, ¹light, and air, are continually [¹ Or water.] begotten in the deep of this world; and that there is no rest or cessation from this begetting; and that it hath been so from the beginning of the world; and yet men can find no cause of it in the outward world, or tell what the ground of it should be: but reason saith, God hath so created it, and therefore it continueth so; which indeed is true in itself; but reason knoweth not the Creator, which doth thus create without ceasing; that is, the true ²*Archæus*, or separator, which is an effluence out [² distinguisher, or divider.] of the invisible world, *viz.* the outflown Word of God; which I mean and understand by the word fiery *Mercury*.

156. For what the invisible world is, in a spiritual working, where light and darkness are in one another, and yet the one not comprehending the other, that the visible world is, in a substantial working; whatsoever powers and virtues in the outflown word are to be ³understood in the inward [³ Or conceived.] spiritual world, the same we understand also in the visible world, in the stars and elements, yet in another Principle of a more holy ⁴nature. [⁴ kind, quality, or condition.]

157. The four elements flow from the *Archæus* of the inward ground, that is, from the four properties of the eternal nature, and were in the beginning of time so outbreathed from the inward ground, and compressed and formed into a working substance and life; and therefore the outward world is called a Principle, and is a subject of the

inward world, that is, a tool and instrument of the inward ¹master, which ¹master is the word and ²power of God.

[margin: ¹ artificer or workman. ² Or virtue.]

158. And as the inward divine world hath in it an ³understanding life from the effluence of the divine knowledge, whereby the angels and souls are meant; so likewise the outward world hath a rational life in it, consisting in the outflown powers and virtues of the inward world; which outward [rational] life hath no higher understanding, and can teach no further than that thing wherein it dwelleth, *viz.* the stars and four elements.

[margin: ³ Or intellectual.]

159. The *spiritus mundi* is hidden in the four elements, as the soul is in the body, and is nothing else but an effluence and working power proceeding from the sun and stars; its dwelling wherein it worketh is spiritual, encompassed with the four elements.

I. 160. The spiritual house is first a sharp magnetical power and virtue, from the effluence of the inward world, from the first property of the eternal nature; this is the ground of all salt and powerful virtue, also of all forming and substantiality.

II. 161. Secondly, it is the effluence of the inward motion, which is outflown from the second ⁴form of the eternal nature, and consisteth in a fiery nature, like a dry kind of water source, which is understood to be the ground of all metal and stones, for they were created of that.

[margin: ⁴ species, kind or property.]

162. I call it the fiery *Mercury* in the spirit of

this world, for it is the mover of all things, and the separator of the powers and virtues; a former of all shapes, a ground of the outward life, as to the motion and sensibility.

163. The third ground is the perception in the motion and sharpness, which is a spiritual source of Sulphur, proceeding from the ground of the painful will in the inward ground: Hence the spirit with the five senses ariseth, *viz.* seeing, hearing, feeling, tasting, and smelling; and is the true essential life, whereby the fire, that is, the fourth form, is made manifest.

III.

164. The ancient wise men have called these three properties *Sulphur*, *Mercurius*, and *Sal*, as to their materials which were produced thereby in the four elements, into which this spirit doth coagulate, or make itself substantial.

165. The four elements lie also in this ground, and are nothing different or several from it; they are only the manifestation of this spiritual ground, and are as a dwelling place of the spirit, in which this spirit worketh.

166. The earth is the grossest effluence from this subtle spirit; after the earth the water is the second; after the water the air is the third; and after the air the fire is the fourth: All these proceed from one only ground, *viz.* from the *spiritus mundi*, which hath its root in the inward world.

167. But reason will say, To what end hath the Creator made this manifestation? I answer, There

is no other cause, but that the spiritual world might thereby bring itself into a visible form or image, that the inward powers and virtues might have a form and image: Now that this might be, the spiritual substance must needs bring itself into a material ground, wherein it may so figure and form itself; and there must be such a separation, as that this separated being might continually long for the first ground again, *viz.* the inward for the outward, and the outward for the inward.

168. So also the four elements, which are nothing else inwardly but one only ground, must long one for the other, and desire one another, and seek the inward ground in one another.

169. For the inward element in them is divided, and the four elements are but the properties of that divided element, and that causeth the great anxiety and desire betwixt them; they will continually [to get] into the first ground again, that is, into that one element in which they may rest; of which the Scripture speaketh, saying: Every creature groaneth with us, and earnestly longeth to be delivered from the vanity, which it is subject unto against its will.

170. In this anxiety and desire, the effluence of the divine power and virtue, by the working of nature, is together also formed and brought into figures, to the eternal glory and contemplation of angels and men, and all eternal creatures; as we may see clearly in all living things, and also in

vegetables, how the divine power and virtue [1] im- [1] fashioneth.
printeth and formeth itself.

171. For there is not anything substantial in this world, wherein the image, resemblance, and form of the inward spiritual world doth not stand; whether it be according to the [2] wrath of the in- [2] Or fierceness. ward ground, or according to the good virtue; and yet in the most [3] venomous virtue or quality, in [3] Or poisonous. the inward ground, many times there lieth the greatest virtue out of the inward world.

172. But where there is a dark life, that is, a dark oil, in a thing, there is little to be expected from it; for it is the foundation of the wrath, *viz.* a false, bad poison, to be utterly rejected.

173. Yet where life consisteth in [4] venom, and [4] Or pain. hath a light or brightness shining in the oil, *viz.* in the fifth essence, therein heaven is manifested in hell, and a great virtue lieth hidden in it: this is understood by those that are ours.

174. The whole visible world is a mere spermatical working ground; every [5] thing hath an [5] Or substance. inclination and longing towards another, the uppermost towards the undermost, and the undermost towards the uppermost, for they are separated one from the other; and in this hunger they embrace one another in the desire.

175. As we may know by the earth, which is so very hungry after the [influence and virtue of the] stars, and the *spiritus mundi*, viz. after the spirit from whence it proceeded in the beginning, that it

hath no rest, for hunger; and this hunger of the earth consumeth bodies, that the spirit may be parted again from the gross elementary ¹condition, and return into its ²*Archæus* again.[^1][^2]

[^1]: Or property.
[^2]: separator, divider, or salnitrous virtue.

176. Also we see in this hunger the impregnation of the *Archæus*, that is, of the separator, how the undermost *Archæus* of the earth attracteth the outermost subtle *Archæus* from the constellations above the earth; where this compacted ground from the uppermost *Archæus* longeth for its ground again, and putteth itself forth towards the uppermost; in which putting forth, the growing of metals, plants and trees, hath its original.

177. For the *Archæus* of the earth becometh thereby exceeding joyful, because it tasteth and feeleth its first ground in itself again, and in this joy all things ³spring out of the earth, and therein also the growing of animals consisteth, *viz.* in a continual conjunction of the heavenly and earthly, in which the divine power and virtue also worketh, as may be known by the tincture of the vegetables in their inward ground.[^3]

[^3]: Or grow.

178. Therefore man, who is so noble an image, having his ground in time and eternity, should well consider himself, and not run headlong in such blindness, seeking his native country afar off from himself, when it is within himself, though covered with the grossness of the elements by their strife.

179. Now when the strife of the elements ceaseth,

by the death of the gross body, then the spiritual man will be made manifest, whether he be born in and to light, or darkness; which of these [two] beareth the sway, and hath the dominion in him, the spiritual man hath his being in it eternally, whether it be in the foundation of God's anger, or in his love.

180. For the outward visible man is not now the image of God, it is nothing but an image of the *Archæus*, that is, a house [or husk] of the spiritual man, in which the spiritual man groweth, as gold doth in the ¹gross stone, and a plant from the wild earth; as the Scripture saith, ²As we have a natural body, so we have also a spiritual body: such as the natural is, such also is the spiritual.

¹ Or drossy stone or ore.
² 1 Cor. xv. 44.

181. The outward gross body of the four elements shall not inherit the kingdom of God, but that which is born out of that one element, *viz.* out of the divine manifestation and working.

182. For this body of the flesh and of the will of man is not it, but that which is wrought by the heavenly *Archæus* in this gross body, unto which this gross [body] is a house, tool, and instrument.

183. But when the crust is taken away, then it shall appear wherefore we have here been called men; and yet some of us have scarce been beasts; nay, some far worse than beasts.

184. For we should rightly consider what the spirit of the outward world is; it is a house, husk, and instrument of the inward spiritual world which

is hidden therein, and worketh through it, and so bringeth itself into figures and images.

185. And thus human reason is but a ¹house of the true understanding of the divine knowledge: none should trust so much in his reason and sharp wit, for it is but the constellation of the outward stars, and doth rather seduce him, than lead him to the Unity of God.

Or dwelling.

186. Reason must wholly yield itself up to God, that the inward *Archæus* may be revealed; and this shall work and bring forth a true spiritual understanding ground, uniform with God, in which God's spirit will be revealed, and will bring the understanding to God: and then, in this ground, ²the spirit searcheth through all things, even the deep things of ³God, as St *Paul* saith.

¹ 1 Cor. ii. 10.
³ Or of the Deity.

187. I thought good to set this down thus briefly for the lovers,⁴ for their further consideration.

⁴ of Mysteries.

⁵*Formula, or Now followeth a short Explication, or* ⁵*Description of the Divine Manifestation.*

model.

188. God is the eternal, *immense, incomprehensible Unity, which manifesteth itself in itself, from eternity in eternity, by the Trinity; and is Father, Son, and Holy Ghost, in a threefold working, as is before mentioned.

189. The first effluence and manifestation of this Trinity is the eternal Word, or outspeaking of the divine power and virtue.

* "immense" (*unmessliche*), "immeasurable."

190. The first outspoken substance from that power is the divine wisdom; which is a substance wherein the power worketh.

191. Out of the wisdom floweth the power and virtue of the breathing forth, and goeth into separability and forming; and therein the divine power is manifest in its virtue.

192. These separable powers and virtues bring themselves * into the power of reception, to their own perceptibility; and out of the perceptibility ariseth own self-will and desire: this own will is the ground of the eternal nature, and it bringeth itself, with the desire, into the properties as far as fire.

193. In the desire is the original of darkness; and in the fire the eternal Unity is made manifest with the light, in the fiery nature.

194. Out of this fiery property, and the property of the light, the angels and souls have their original; which is a divine manifestation.

195. The power and virtue of fire and light is called tincture; and the motion of this virtue is called the holy and pure element.

196. The darkness becometh substantial in itself; and the light becometh also substantial in the fiery desire: these two make two Principles, *viz.* God's anger in the darkness, and God's love in the light; each of them worketh in itself, and there is only

---

* "into the power of reception, to their own perceptibility" (*Selbst-Empfindlichkeit*), or "into receptibility to self-perceptibility."

such a difference between them, as between day and night, and yet both of them have but one only ground; and the one is always a cause of the other, and that the other becometh manifest and known in it, as light from fire.

197. The visible world is the third Principle, that is, the third ground and beginning: this is outbreathed out of the inward ground, *viz.* out of both the first Principles, and brought into the nature and form of a creature.

198. The inward eternal working is hidden in the visible world; and it is in everything, and through everything, yet not to be comprehended by anything in the thing's own power; the outward powers and virtues are but passive, and the house in which the inward work.

199. [1] All the other worldly creatures are but the substance of the outward world, but man, who is created both out of time and eternity, out of the Being of all beings, and made an image of the divine manifestation.

[1] The common creatures.

200. The eternal manifestation of the divine light is called the kingdom of heaven, and the habitation of the holy angels and souls.

201. The fiery darkness is called hell, or God's anger, wherein the devils dwell, together with the damned souls.

202. In the place of this world, heaven and hell are present everywhere, but according to the inward ground.

203. Inwardly, the divine working is manifest in God's children; but in the wicked, the working of the painful darkness.

204. The place of the eternal paradise is hidden in this world, in the inward ground; but manifest in the inward man, in which God's power and virtue worketh.

205. There shall perish of this world only the four elements, together with the starry heaven, and the earthly creatures, *viz.* the outward gross life of all things.

206. The inward power and virtue of every substance remaineth eternally.

Another Exposition of [1] *the* Mysterium magnum.

[1] The Great Mystery.

207. God hath manifested the *Mysterium magnum* out of the power and virtue of his Word; in which *Mysterium magnum* the whole creation hath lain essentially without forming, in *temperamento*; and by which he hath outspoken the spiritual formings in separability [or variety]: in which formings, the sciences of the powers and virtues in the desire, that is, in the *Fiat*, have stood, wherein every science, in the desire to manifestation, hath brought itself into a corporeal substance.

208. Such a *Mysterium magnum* lieth also in man, *viz.* in the image of God, and is the essential Word of the power of God, according to time and eternity, by which the living Word of God out-

speaketh, or expresseth itself, either in love or anger, or in fancy, all as the *Mysterium* standeth in a movable desire to evil or good; according to that saying, Such as the people is, such a God they also have.

209. For in whatsoever properties the *Mysterium* in man is awakened, such a word also uttereth itself from his powers: as we plainly see that nothing else but vanity is uttered by the wicked. *Praise the Lord, all ye his works. Hallelujah.*

Of the Word [1]SCIENCE.

[1] SCIENTZ.

210. The word Science is not so taken by me as men understand the word *scientia* in the *Latin* tongue; for I understand therein even the true ground according to sense, which, both in the *Latin* and all other languages is missed and neglected by ignorance; for every word in its impressure, forming, and expression, gives the true understanding of what that thing is that is so called.

211. You understand by Science some skill or knowledge, in which you say true, but do not fully express the meaning.

212. Science is the root to the understanding, as to the [2]sensibility; it is the root to the centre of the [3]impressure of nothing into something; as when the will of the abyss attracteth itself into itself, to a centre of the impressure, *viz.* to the word, then ariseth the true understanding.

[2] cogitation, consideration, or reasoning.
[3] Or forming.

213. The will is in the separability of the Science, and there separateth itself out from the impressed compaction; and men first of all understand the essence in that which is separated, in which the separability impresseth itself into a substance.

214. For ¹essence is a substantial power and virtue, but Science is a moving flitting one, like the senses; it is indeed the root of the senses.   ¹ ESSENTZ.

215. Yet in the understanding, in which it is called Science, it is not the sensing, but a cause of the sensing, in that manner as when the understanding *impresseth itself in the mind, there must first be a cause which must †give the mind, from which the understanding floweth forth into its contemplation: Now this Science is the root to the fiery mind, and it is in short the root of all spiritual beginnings; it is the true root of souls, and proceedeth through every life, for it is the ground from whence life cometh.

216. I could not give it any other better name, this doth so wholly accord and agree in the sense; for the Science is the cause that the divine abyssal will compacteth and impresseth itself into nature, to the separable [various], intelligible, and perceivable life of understanding and difference; for from the impressure of the Science, whereby the will attracteth it into itself,

* "impresseth itself" (*fasset sich*), or "concretes itself."
† "give the mind," or "produce," "give rise to the mind."

* the natural life ariseth, and the word of every life originally.

217. The distinction or separation out of the fire is to be understood as followeth: The eternal Science in the will of the Father draweth the will, which is called Father, into itself, and shutteth itself into a centre of the divine generation of the Trinity, and by the Science speaketh itself forth into a word of understanding; and in the speaking is the separation in the Science; and in every separation there is the desire to the impressure of the [1] expression, the impressure is essential, and is called divine essence.

[1] Or out-speaking.

218. From this essence the word expresseth itself in the second separation, that is, of nature, and in that expression (wherein the natural will separateth itself in its centre, into a sensing), the separation out of the fiery [2] Science is understood; for thence cometh the soul and all angelical spirits.

[2] One copy hath essence.

219. The third separation is according to the outward nature of the expressed formed word, wherein the bestial Science lieth, as may be seen in the treatise of the *Election of Grace*, which hath [3] a sharp understanding, and is one of the clearest of our writings.

[3] acute, or sublime.

* "the natural life ariseth," etc., or, "originateth the natural life, and the word of every life [or all life]."

FINIS

A CATALOGUE OF THE BOOKS WRITTEN BY JACOB BEHMEN

1. *Anno* 1612. He wrote the first book called *Aurora, the Rising of the Sun*, and he, being accused as author thereof, this book was laid up by the Magistrate at Görlitz, at Court, and command given him that he should henceforth (being a simple layman) refrain writing of books, which did not belong to his profession and condition. Whereupon he did refrain for seven years, but afterwards, being stirred up again by the Holy Spirit of God, and also being encouraged thereto by the entreaty and desires of some people that feared God, he betook himself to his pen again, and proceeded in writing, and perfected, with good leisure and deliberation, the rest which follow, viz. :
2. *Anno* 1619. The second book, *Of the Three Principles*, together with *An Appendix of the Threefold Life of Man*.
3. *Anno* 1620. A book of the *Threefold Life of Man*.
4. An Answer to the *Forty Questions of the Soul*, propounded by Doctor Balthasar Walter. In the first chapter of it is an Exposition of the *Turned Eye*, or *Philosophic Globe*, with an addition concerning the soul, the image of the soul, and the turba or destroyeress of the image.
5. Three Books: The first, *Of the Incarnation of Jesus Christ*. The second, *Of the Suffering, Death, and Resurrection of Christ*. The third, *Of the Tree of Faith*.
6. A book of *Six Points*.
7. A book of *The Heavenly and Earthly Mysterium*.
8. A book of *The Last Times*. To P. K.
9. *Anno* 1621. A book, *De Signatura Rerum*, or *The Signature of all Things*.

10. A consolatory book, *Of the Four Complexions.*
11. *An Apology to Balthasar Tilken,* in two parts.
12. *A Consideration upon Esaias Stiefel's Book.*
13. *Anno 1622.* A book, *Of True Repentance.*
14. A book, *Of True Resignation.*
15. A book, *Of Regeneration.*
16. *Anno 1623.* A book, *Of Predestination and Election of God.* At the end of it is written the following treatise, viz. :—
17. *A Short Compendium of Repentance.*
18. *The Mysterium Magnum.* Upon *Genesis.*
19. *Anno 1624. A Table of the Principles,* or a *Key* of his writings. To G. F. and I. H.
20. A little book, *Of the Supersensual Life.*
(21.) A little book, *Of Divine Contemplation.*
22. A book, *Of the Two Testaments of Christ,* viz. *Baptism and the Supper of the Lord.*
23. *A Dialogue between the Enlightened and the Unenlightened Soul.*
24. *An Apology upon the Book of True Repentance.* Directed against a Pasquil of the principal minister of Görlitz, called Gregory Rickter.
(25.) A book of *177 Theosophic Questions.*
26. *An Epitome of the Mysterium Magnum.*
(27.) *The Holy Week,* or *The Prayer Book.*
28. *A Table of the Divine Manifestation,* or *An Exposition of the Threefold World.* To I. S. V. S. and A. V. F.

In these two that follow the date is not set down.

29. A book, *Of the Errors of the Sects of Ezechiel Meths.* To A. P. A., or *An Apology to Esaias Stiefel.*
30. A book, *Of the Last Judgment.*

Further:

31. Certain *Letters to Divers Persons.* Written at divers times, with certain *Keys* for some hidden words.

The books which the author finished not, are marked with this sign ( ).